15 Surefire SCRIPTS

LAMB'S PLAYERS PRESENTS

15 Surefire SCRIPTS

for a Variety of Church Settings

Edited by Kerry Cederberg Meads &
Robert Smyth

World Wide Publications
A ministry of the Billy Graham Evangelistic Association
1303 Hennepin Ave., Minneapolis, MN 55403

Fifteen Surefire Scripts

©1989 Lamb's Players

All rights reserved. No part of this publication may be reproduced in any form without written permission from the publisher: World Wide Publications, 1303 Hennepin Avenue, Minneapolis, Minnesota 55403.

World Wide Publications is the publishing ministry of the Billy Graham Evangelistic Association.

Scripture quotations are taken from the King James Version, the New International Version (Copyright © 1973, 1978, 1984 International Bible Society. Used by permission of Zondervan Bible Publishers), and the New American Standard Version (© 1960, 1962, 1963, 1968, 1971, 1972, 1973, 1975, 1977 The Lockman Foundation, La Habra, California).

ISBN: 0-89066-186-3

Library of Congress Catalog Card Number: 89-050949

Printed in the United States of America

Contents

Introduction 7

Topical Sketches 9

  1. The Super-Deluxe Christian Life Success Kit 11
  2. The Authority Inspector 17
  3. Stuff 25
  4. Fishers of Men 33
  5. Morning, Bill! 39
  6. Is It More Blessed to Give Than Receive? 47
  7. Dave and Bruce 53

Story Theater 59

  8. David and Goliath 61
  9. The Three Little Pigs and the Architect 73
  10. The Farmer, the Soldier, and the Prisoner 83
  11. The Parable of the Assignments 91

Choral Readings 99

  12. The Glory of the Lord 101
  13. Our Weakness, His Strength 109
  14. The Lord's Unfailing Love 115
  15. Serve the Lord With Gladness 121

Introduction

The church is discovering the dramatic arts.

And it's ironic, because that's where it all began. Western theater started in the church. Its first actors were clergy. Its first scripts were Scripture. The Church found drama to be a powerful means of communication. It was an aid to teaching and to worship. Congregations swelled when drama was presented.

A lot of years passed. Somewhere along the line the baby got tossed out with the bathwater; a big chunk of the church gave up on drama—and the rest of the arts. (Except for certain types of music!)

Happily, things are beginning to come full-circle. The church is rediscovering the dramatic arts. What we have in this collection are some offerings which we hope, in their own little way, will aid in that larger rediscovery.

While the scripts in this book present a wide variety of styles and themes, they do have some things in common—

> They are short (five to ten minutes).
> They are easy to present (small casts, flexible staging, few props).
> They are versatile (you can adjust them to fit your people and your space).

And they have been put to the test. They have all been performed—in different situations—before audiences numbering from twelve to ten thousand. Some are great for youth meetings or as discussion starters. Some work best as introductions or illustrations to sermons. The choral readings make a nice addition to a worship service. We even used one in a wedding!

Now, you give them a try. Get some committed, excited people together. Remember the Creator you serve. Put your best efforts into it. Use your imagination, and offer some of these as a gift to your audience.

It is our prayer that these will give you the inspiration to write your own!

Performance Rights

All the scripts in this book may be performed without royalty payments providing all the following conditions are met:

1) they are not performed in any situation where a fee is charged
2) they are not performed by a professional performance group
3) any printed program or bulletin must include this information:

(Script title) by (Author), from Lamb's Players Presents, 15 Surefire Scripts *published by World Wide Publications.*

For performance rights in situations other than the above, contact:

Lamb's Players, PO Box 26, National City, CA 92050

About Lamb's Players

Since its founding in 1971, Lamb's Players has pioneered a Christian voice in the dramatic arts. A professional non-profit organization, Lamb's Players is a full-time ensemble of actors, designers, directors and playwrights exploring the integration of the Christian faith and the dramatic arts. Lamb's Players Theatre, the ensemble's resident stage in San Diego, California, maintains a year-round production schedule. Its touring companies have performed internationally to well over a million people.

The Contributors

Wayne Harrell lives in Portland, Oregon and writes and performs with Proverbial Players.

Carol Henegar received her M.A. in Directing from San Diego State University. A lover of reader's theater, she toured for many years with Lamb's Players Touring Company.

Kerry Cederberg Meads is an associate director with Lamb's Players. She wears the many hats of actor, director, literary manager and playwright.

Deborah Gilmour Smyth is an associate director with Lamb's Players. A long standing member of their resident repertory company, she also enjoys adapting material for choral reading and reader's theater.

Robert Smyth, is the producing artistic director of Lamb's Players. An actor and director, he also enjoys writing when he can find the time.

Judy Urschel is the director and primary scriptwriter for the Proverbial Players in Portland, Oregon.

For more in-depth information on starting or developing a drama ministry, look for *Lamb's Players Presents - How to Develop a Drama Group*, also published by World Wide Publications.

Topical Sketches

1

The Super-Deluxe Christian Life Success Kit

by
Robert Smyth

THEME: The world's way to success vs. God's way.

RUNNING TIME: Six minutes

CAST:

Guy: nothing special about him, just your average kind of guy
Salesperson #1: hyper, aggressive, fast-talking, flashy sales-type
Salesperson #2: hyper, aggressive, fast-talking, flashy sales-type
Salesperson #3: hyper, aggressive, fast-talking, flashy sales-type
Rescue: very normal, nothing flashy about him or her

PRODUCTION SUGGESTIONS:

Props:
   Large suitcase labeled "THE LOOK"
   Large suitcase labeled "WORDS"
   Large suitcase labeled "$ THINGS $"
   Large suitcase labeled "CONDEMNATION"
   Large suitcase labeled "PRIDE"
   List on a piece of paper

Costumes:
   Salepersons #s 1, 2, and 3: dressed in suits with flashy colors or plaids to give them a comic flair
   Guy and Rescue: normal, everyday street clothes

The Super-Deluxe Christian Life Success Kit
THE SCRIPT

GUY

(Entering) Hi! I've got to tell you how excited I am to be a Christian. I'm learning so much. But I was thinking, maybe there's some special key to all of this. You see, what I really want to know is this—what is it I need to lead a truly successful Christian life?

(Trio of hyper sales-types burst onto the scene with their wares.)

SALESPERSON #1

Soooo, you say you want to be a successful Christian, do you? Well, son, I say, son, step right up. For you, my boy, have come to just the right place. I say, the right place.

SALESPERSON #2

We've got it!

SALESPERSON #3

Just what you need to get to the top!

SALESPERSON #1

Special for you!

SALESPERSON #2

On sale today only!

SALESPERSON #3

The super-deluxe, go anywhere, impress anyone, worldly wise, Christian life success kit!

GUY

Well, I . . .

SALESPERSON #1

Now you want to be successful in this walk of yours, don't ya? Well, don't ya?

GUY

Well, yes.

SALESPERSON #1

Then listen up, my boy, and listen up good. This kit has all you need. Yes sir, look no further. It's all right here.

SALESPERSON #2

Tsk, tsk, the first thing we have to change is your look. Must have the right *Look*. And in here you'll find it all. *(Slings a piece of luggage with "The Look" onto him.)* Your Sunday suit, your never-droop smile, your smartly trimmed hair. And, . . . seventeen pounds of cross, fish, and dove jewelry along with numerous assorted 3-D witnessing items.

SALESPERSON #1

Now, son, the next thing you need to be truly successful is com-mun-i-ca-tion. That's right. Communication. And the most important part of communication is to talk. What you need are *Words*. *(Slings "Words" bag on him.)* That's right, words, words, and plenty of them. Big words. Grand words. Emotional words. Intellectual words—multi-syllabic wonders! Remember, never listen—always talk. Why, you'll have an answer for everything! And, son, remember—never stop talking!

SALESPERSON #3

Whoa, whoa, whoa! But how do you expect to be heard if people don't respect you? Listen to me, my friend. Now to be a true worldly wise Christian in today's world, you need to impress people. That's what gets their respect—envy even. How do you do that, you ask? Why, with good *Things!* That's right. Things. Toys, stuff, possessions! *(Slings on "$ Things $" bag.)* More and more things—*that* will get you respect. Why, you'll have people eating out of your hand!

SALESPERSON #2

Listen, listen, listen! You're on your way. Success isn't far off. But there are a few more things you need. To be really successful you need to know how to throw a good punch. Identify the enemy and destroy him. Show no mercy, show no love! What you need is a good dose of *Condemnation! (Pile on "Condemnation" bag.)* Glorious, hateful condemnation—make 'em quiver! And remember, in the Christian army we shoot our wounded!

SALESPERSON #1

And, finally, my boy, one crowning virtue to help you through the hard times.

SALESPERSON #2

Have this and you have it all.

SALESPERSON #3

The last piece in the Super-Deluxe Worldly Wise Christian Life Success Kit.

SALESPERSON #2

Above all else, remember how important YOU are.

SALESPERSON #3

You deserve the very best!

SALESPERSON #2

You're above all the rest!

SALESPERSON #1

Son, have a good old-fashioned dose of *Pride!* *(Last bag of "Pride" piled on, and Guy is now staggering with his burden)*

RESCUE

(Enters other side)

Pssssst.

GUY

Huh?

RESCUE

Pssssssst!

GUY

Excuse me, somebody's "pssssssting" me.

RESCUE

Over here. *(Guy takes a step toward her.)* That's right, over here! Flee!

GUY

What?

RESCUE

That way leads to destruction—it's the enemy's way. Flee, run, get away. *(Guy is hesitant.)* Drop it all, and run from it! NOW!

(Guy drops all the baggage and goes to her.)

SALESPEOPLE #1,2,3

Hey!

GUY

Well, if all of that's not what I need to be a success, what is?

RESCUE

This. (*Hands him a list*)

GUY

(*Reads*) "Maturity in the Word, compassion, perseverance, gentleness, integrity." Can I get these from you?

RESCUE

No, sorry. See, they're not for sale. But follow after Christ, be a reflection of God's love, and they will be given to you from above. Remember—flee, follow, and fight the good fight.

GUY

Flee, follow, and fight the good fight.

RESCUE

That's it!

RESCUE AND GUY

Flee, follow, and fight the good fight.

(*They exit, repeating the phrase in rhythm.*)

SALESPEOPLE #1,2,3

(*Exiting through the audience, talking as they go*)

How about you? Special today. We've got just what you need! (*ETC.*)

2

The Authority Inspector

by
Robert Smyth

THEME: The authority of the Word of God (works best as an introduction to a sermon or lesson)

RUNNING TIME: Five minutes

CAST:

Authority Inspector: very efficient
Warm-Up: charismatic and energetic
Speaker #1: intensely emotional
Speaker #2: staunch, and strait-laced
Speaker #3: intellectual and scholarly

PRODUCTION SUGGESTIONS:

The Inspector works best when played with a British accent.

Props:
    Badge
    Small pad that has pages that can be ripped out
    Pen or pencil
    Stack of books

Costumes:
    Authority Inspector: some kind of uniform and/or hat
    Warm-Up: a jogging outfit
    Speaker #1: regular street clothes
    Speaker #2: dressed in his/her Sunday best
    Speaker #3: dressed collegiately, with glasses perhaps

The Authority Inspector
THE SCRIPT

WARM-UP

(Comes up onto the stage through the audience with vitality and takes total control of the audience.)

All right, all right! Let's go! Everybody up. That's right, on your feet. We don't want any of you falling asleep on us. Let's get that blood circulating—keep our minds fresh.

(Leads the audience in a variety of physical exercises)

All together now. Hands up over your heads and reach—reach. Come on. All right, down.

(The Authority Inspector enters and watches the action.)

Now, shake hands with the person on either side of you. Okay, okay, that's enough. Now let's raise our right arms out in front—

INSPECTOR

Excuse me.

WARM-UP

And swing it in a slow arc—

INSPECTOR

Excuse me.

WARM-UP

Yes?

INSPECTOR

Excuse me. But just what, exactly, are you doing?

WARM-UP

Why, I'm waking everybody up. We don't want people snoring at us.

INSPECTOR

I see. And, may I ask, by what authority are you doing this?

WARM-UP

What?

INSPECTOR

You see, I am an Authority Inspector. *(Shows his badge)*

WARM-UP

An Authority Inspector?

INSPECTOR

Yes. And so I must ask you again, by what authority are you doing this?

WARM-UP

Well . . . I guess . . . I just thought it was a good idea.

INSPECTOR

I see. You just thought it was a good idea?

WARM-UP

Uh-huh.

INSPECTOR

Sorry, invalid authority! *(Whips out his notebook and writes a ticket)* I must issue you an Authority Violation Citation. Please leave the stage immediately.

WARM-UP

But I—*(Exiting)*

INSPECTOR

That's right, thank you. Goodbye. You may all be seated.

(The audience sits.)

Thank you. You see, today, people don't seem to understand the need for proper authority. That's why my job as an Authority Inspector is so important.

SPEAKER #1

(Entering from the opposite side, takes podium or pulpit, and starts speaking in midthought)

I have ached for the chaos around us. I look at our world today in horror and disbelief. And so, friends, I want to tell you truthfully, from my heart, that you must change your way of thinking. You must—

INSPECTOR

Excuse me.

SPEAKER #1

You must change your behavior, you—

INSPECTOR

Excuse me. *(Showing his badge)* Authority Inspector here. By what authority do you speak?

SPEAKER #1

By what authority do I speak?

INSPECTOR

Correct.

SPEAKER #1

Well, I . . . I speak because I feel that I should. And I feel that what I have to say is important. And I feel—

INSPECTOR

Would you say then that your authority is your feelings?

SPEAKER #1

Why yes, my authority is my feelings!

INSPECTOR

Sorry. That's all very nice, but—*(Writing out another ticket)* invalid authority for proclamation! Here is your Authority Violation Citation. Please leave the stage. *(Speaker #1 exits.)*
That's right, move right along. Thank you. Good thing I'm on the job today!

SPEAKER #2

(Entering) And so, once again I stand before you. I am here to comfort you, to reassure you. To remind you that what we have done this past year we will do again this coming year. All things are orderly and in their proper place.

INSPECTOR

(Showing his badge) Excuse me. Authority Inspector here. I must ask you, by what authority do you speak?

SPEAKER #2

Me? Well, I speak because it's always been done—that's just the way the church does things. It's tradition!

INSPECTOR

I see.

SPEAKER #2

Tradition is my authority.

INSPECTOR

So sorry. *(Writing out the ticket)* Invalid authority for proclamation. Your citation, thank you. Kindly leave the stage. *(Speaker #2 exits.)* Quite a full day we're having!

SPEAKER #3

(Entering with a stack of books) And, therefore, I ask, "How can you come to any other conclusion?" We have seen the truth of it in Augustine, in Luther, in Wesley, and in Calvin. We have looked at Keil and Dalich. We have the enlightened thoughts of Nietzsche, of Sagan, of Doonsbury! Need I say more?

INSPECTOR

Excuse me. *(Showing his badge)* Authority Inspector here.

SPEAKER #3

Yes, what is it?

INSPECTOR

Brief question. By what authority do you speak?

SPEAKER #3

Ah, now you look like someone who can appreciate authority.

INSPECTOR

Quite so.

SPEAKER #3

You see, I stand on the best! I saturate my mind with fact and opinion—my library is unmatched! Why, the experts are my authority.

INSPECTOR

No, sorry. *(Writing out the ticket)* Invalid authority for proclamation. Your citation. That will be all, thank you. *(Speaker #3 exits)* Disappointing, isn't it? Now, is there no one here who can provide us with the correct authority for proclamation?

(Lead into the lesson or sermon)

3

Stuff

by
Judy Urschel

THEME: "Lay not up for yourselves treasures upon earth, where moth and rust doth corrupt, and where thieves break through and steal: But lay up for yourselves treasures in heaven, where neither moth nor rust doth corrupt, and where thieves do not break through nor steal: For where your treasure is, there will your heart be also." (Matthew 6:19-21, KJV)

RUNNING TIME: Seven minutes

CAST:

Bruce: constant organizer and reorganizer of all his stuff
Pam: the ultimate sale fanatic
Jean and Ron: a pair of garage-sale shoppers
Wayne: saves everything, can't throw a thing away
Karen: the grocery shopper, coupon savings are her life
Martha: a junk collector
Gabriel: (*an offstage voice*) the angelic flight attendant

All characters are more interested in their stuff than in anything else in the world.

PRODUCTION SUGGESTIONS:

Props:
    Offstage microphone for Gabriel
    Bruce's stuff: lots of boxes in all shapes and sizes piled all over the stage
    Pam's stuff: as many wrapped packages and big shopping bags as she can possibly carry
    Jean and Ron's stuff: lots of odd-shaped things wrapped in newspaper, which they can barely carry

Wayne's stuff: dusty crates, trunks, and garment bags that have been stored in the attic
Karen's stuff: as many grocery bags as she can carry, filled to the brim
Martha's stuff: big plastic garbage bags she has to drag in with her

All of the "stuff" should be as non-specific as possible. The audience will mentally fill the boxes and bags with their own "stuff."

Style:
The pacing should be lively and quick. The characters should be constantly working with their "stuff."

Stuff
THE SCRIPT

Bruce is on stage organizing stacks of boxes all over the place—a good-sized mess. Pam comes in loaded down with bags from a shoppingtrip, looking for space to put all her stuff. Neither of them really look at each other as they're talking. The other characters should enter from different locations as much as possible, so as to denote them coming from different places. They can be talking as they come down the aisle.)

PAM

You wouldn't believe all the stuff they had on sale today!

BRUCE

I didn't know there was a sale on.

PAM

Oh sure, just look in the paper. It was in that section that had those horrible pictures of that earthquake.

BRUCE

Sad, isn't it? All those people losing all their earthly belongings with a single blow

PAM

Yeah. Anyway, I just couldn't decide what to buy, so I got it all. Wait until you see it!

BRUCE

Well, don't put it down over there. That's all my stuff.

PAM

Why do you have your stuff spread out all over the place?

BRUCE

I'm organizing it.

PAM

(Looking inside a box) This looks pretty worthless. Is this all the stuff you're going to throw away?

BRUCE

No! That's all the stuff that I don't need right now but I might need someday.

PAM

Oh. Well, what about this stuff?

BRUCE

That's all the stuff I've organized.

PAM

What about this stuff?

BRUCE

That's all the stuff I'm *going* to organize.

PAM

I've got to put my stuff down *somewhere.*

BRUCE

If you're going to be that way about it. *(Moves one small box grudgingly. Jean and Ron enter loaded with odd-sized packages wrapped in newspaper.)*

RON

That had to be the garage sale of all garage sales! You made some great deals!

JEAN

Well, they had to sell everything, didn't they? I mean with the bank foreclosing on them, they need every penny they can get. I mean they can't eat this stuff.

RON

And then when you made an offer on that necklace the woman was wearing—

JEAN

I think it just might be an antique that's worth quite a lot.

RON

I wish I had your nerve.

JEAN

Oh, it'll come to you. All you need is a little practice.

BRUCE

You're not going to try and put all your stuff in here are you?

JEAN

Who died and left you boss?

BRUCE

Oh, stuff it!

JEAN

We live here the same as you!

RON

Besides, this is just an empty box sitting right here.

BRUCE

No it isn't. That's the box for the stuff that was stolen last week when we were burglarized.

RON

Oh yeah. Do you suppose we'll ever see that stuff again?

PAM

I'm not taking any chances. From now on I'm buying two of everything!

JEAN

Well can't we at least move it over here?

BRUCE

Yeah, I guess so. *(Again moves something very grudgingly)*

WAYNE

(Has dragged in a huge trunk) All right. Who forgot to put the mothballs in all the stuff in the attic?

JEAN

Not me.

RON

That wasn't my job.

BRUCE

(To Pam) I thought you were going to do that.

PAM

Me?

WAYNE

Oh, just forget it. Look at it—some of this stuff is absolutely ruined!

RON

Just put it over there with the stuff that Bruce is going to fix.

PAM

We don't have any more room in here. You'll have to put your stuff out in the garage.

WAYNE

Not me, man, no way! Everything I stored out there got wet and grew green and purple with mold or rusted into pieces.

KAREN

(Enters with as many grocery bags as she can carry) Gang way! The greatest coupon shopper of the world has returned! I covered every store in the area, used every coupon we had in the house, and saved more money than most people earn in a week. Boy, it's stuffy in here!

BRUCE

I hope you're not planning on putting any of that stuff in here because we don't have any more room.

JEAN

If you moved some of your stuff then maybe we wouldn't have that problem.

WAYNE

(Has gone out and come back in again with another huge trunk or box, tripping over some of the other stuff as he comes) For once I'd like to be able to get at my own stuff without tripping over everyone else's.

PAM

I told you there was plenty of room in the garage.

MARTHA

(Comes in dragging her stuff) Look at this! I got some great stuff that the people down the street were just going to throw away! This is practically brand new. And I just fell in love with this. And—*(Everyone starts pushing and grabbing and demanding some of Martha's stuff. After a few seconds of this, there is the sound effect of an "airplane announcement tone," at which point all the characters stop and listen.)*

GABRIEL

(Offstage) Ladies and gentlemen, may I have your attention, please. This is the final boarding call for Flight 777, non-stop service to New Jerusalem on Paradise Airways. Our regulations do prohibit any carry-on luggage and for your convenience, none of our planes have baggage compartments. *(The characters slowly move off the stage in shock.)* So sit back, relax, and enjoy the trip to your final destination. My name is Gabriel and I'll be your flight attendant today.

4

Fishers of Men

by
Kerry Cederberg Meads

THEME: The importance of discipleship in building up the body of Christ

RUNNING TIME: Six minutes

CAST:

Uncle Paul: a fisherman
John Mark: around twelve to fourteen years old, Uncle Paul's nephew
Timmy: around five to eight years old, also Uncle Paul's nephew

PRODUCTION SUGGESTIONS:

Set:
   The stage should be full of fishing equipment: fishing rods, nets, buckets, tackle boxes, lures, etc.

Props:
   Fishing rod that is functional for Uncle Paul
   Fishing rod, bucket with empty stringer inside, tackle box, net, and fishing book for John Mark
   Bamboo pole or stick with a string attached to it

Costumes:
   Uncle Paul: dressed like a seasoned fisherman complete with vest, hat, waders, boots, etc.
   John Mark: dressed the same as his uncle, but all his clothing is too large for him
   Timmy: jeans, T-shirt, and baseball cap

Fishers of Men
THE SCRIPT

(Uncle Paul comes on stage whistling, "I Will Make You Fishers of Men," and begins to practice casting.)

UNCLE PAUL

(Directly to audience) I love to fish. . . . love to fish. . . . Always have—always will. . . . Been doing it for years. There's something about being out on the water waiting for that nibble. It takes patience—a lot of patience. But when you get that bite and reel that fish in . . . well, I can just imagine what old Peter felt like when Jesus said, "I will make you fishers of men." Yeah. The waiting also gives me time to "catch up" on my memorization. *(He quickly and proudly recites.)* Ephesians 4:11-14: "It was he who gave some to be apostles, some to be prophets, some to be evangelists, and some to be pastors and teachers, to prepare God's people for works of service, so that the body of Christ may be built up until we all reach unity in the faith and in the knowledge of the Son of God and become mature, attaining to the whole measure of the fullness of Christ." *(John Mark enters, laden with fishing equipment, as his Uncle Paul continues reciting)* "Then we will no longer be infants, tossed back and forth by the waves, and blown here and there by every wind of teaching and by the cunning and craftiness of men . . ."

(John Mark drops all of his equipment with a loud crash. Uncle Paul turns to look.)

Well, looky here. This is my nephew, John Mark—my brother's boy. He loves to fish, just like me. I brought him with me once a few years ago. That's all it took and he was "hooked." The boy really looks up to me. I'm his favorite uncle—sort of a role model, I guess.

(By this time John Mark is sitting slumped on a bucket.)

He's bright, motivated, and has unlimited energy—
(John Mark sighs)

Usually. Ah, he seems kind of disappointed. Excuse me a moment, would you?

(Turns his attention to John Mark)

Hello, John Mark.

(No response from John Mark, so Uncle Paul tries to cast over to him several times to try and get his attention.)

Didn't catch any fish, eh?

(John Mark lifts up a chain without any fish on it and lets it fall back into the bucket.)

JOHN MARK

Uncle Paul, I was out there for *five* hours!

UNCLE PAUL

Well, John Mark, maybe it's just not your gift.

JOHN MARK

But, Uncle Paul, I *love* being out there, and I'm patient. I wait, but it gets kind of discouraging.

UNCLE PAUL

Did you read that book I gave you?

JOHN MARK

Yes. I read it the minute you gave it to me, but reading about it and doing it are two different things. I mean, some of it was kind of hard to understand. I asked some of the men hanging around down by the lake about it. One said my problem was that I wasn't using live bait. But this other guy said it didn't matter and another told me my line was too thick. Then another said I was using the wrong lure—that I needed something more flashy. I don't know which one to believe.

UNCLE PAUL

I know, I know. You've got to be discerning. Every one of those guys has their own "fish story" and it can be confusing.

JOHN MARK

Well, that's when I thought that maybe you could take me along with you—so I could learn firsthand.

(Uncle Paul clears his throat and fidgets apprehensively.)

I promise I'll be quiet—I won't scare the fish. I'll just watch—"on the job training," so to speak. You know what they say, "Experience is the best teacher."

UNCLE PAUL

Yes, well, you just keep going on your own and you'll gain experience . . . on your own.

JOHN MARK

But I could learn a lot from how you handle different situations—unless you want to keep it all to yourself.

UNCLE PAUL

Now, now, that's not it John Mark.

JOHN MARK

That's okay Uncle Paul, I can see you have a lot of important things on your mind and having me around would just slow you down.

UNCLE PAUL

That's really adult of you to understand, John Mark.

(Uncle Paul gathers his equipment and realizes that he can't carry it all.)

JOHN MARK

I'll just run over to the neighbors. I hear he's a great fisherman.

UNCLE PAUL

A great fisherman, huh?

JOHN MARK

Some people say he's the *best*.

UNCLE PAUL

The best?

JOHN MARK

The *very* best. I think he likes me. Maybe he'll take me along with him. I heard he holds the record for the most gigantic—

UNCLE PAUL

On second thought, maybe it's time I share some of my practical knowledge with you—that's something you can't get out of books.

JOHN MARK

I promise I'll stay out of the way.

UNCLE PAUL

Now, don't you worry about that. Hands on experience is the best way to learn. I think you'll be a big help. Why don't you start by carrying that right over there.

JOHN MARK

(Going to get the equipment) You'll see, I'll be one of the best investments you ever made!

TIMMY

(Running onto the stage with his bamboo pole) Uncle Paul, Uncle Paul! Will you take me fishing too?

UNCLE PAUL

Ah, this is my other nephew—my sister's boy, Timmy.

TIMMY

You're my *favorite* uncle.

JOHN MARK

I'll take care of it, Uncle Paul. *(To Timmy)* I tell you what—there's only room for two in the boat, but after Uncle Paul teaches me, I'll pass everything I learn on to you. You can start out with this book.

(John Mark gives Timmy the fishing book out of his back pocket. All exit whistling "I Will Make You Fishers of Men.")

5

Morning, Bill!

by
Robert Smyth

THEME: The irony of our "fan"atical expressions

RUNNING TIME: Five minutes

CAST:

Bill: warm, bright personality
Jerry: very gregarious
Waitress: polite and conscientious

PRODUCTION SUGGESTIONS:

Set:
    Table and chairs for two
    Red checked tablecloth

Props:
    Pad and pencil for waitress
    Two menus
    Coffee pot
    Two cups of coffee
    Two plates with eggs and bacon with toast on the side
    Two sets of forks, knives, and spoons
    Salt and pepper shakers
    Flower in a vase

Keep all waitress stuff just upstage of Bill and Jerry, so she can move quickly.

Another option is to use two chairs and mime all set pieces and props.

Costumes:
- Everyday street clothes for Bill and Jerry
- White blouse, dark skirt, and white apron for waitress

Style:
- Insert the names of local football players in the appropriate blank spaces

Morning, Bill!
THE SCRIPT

(The scene opens with Bill sitting at the table, drinking a cup of coffee in the restaurant. The waitress enters to take his order)

WAITRESS

Have you decided?

BILL

Yes. I'd like the Number Two, please.

WAITRESS

How would you like your eggs?

BILL

Sunnyside up.

WAITRESS

White, whole wheat, or rye toast?

BILL

Whole wheat, please.

WAITRESS

Thank you. *(Exits)*

JERRY

(Enters with a burst of energy) Morning, Bill!

BILL

Hi, Jer.

JERRY

Been waiting long? *(Sits and picks up the menu)*

BILL

Just got here five minutes ago.

JERRY

Ordered yet?

BILL

Yeah, go ahead.

WAITRESS

(Entering with coffee pot) Good morning, sir. Coffee? *(Pours Jerry a cup)*

JERRY

Sure thing! And, uh, let's see. Give me this Number Two with the eggs over easy, and the bacon well done—just this side of burnt. And an English muffin instead of toast. Oh, and grape jelly. You've got grape jelly, don't ya?

WAITRESS

Yes, sir. *(Taking his menu, she exits.)*

JERRY

(Becoming more excited) Hey, Bill, did you catch that game yesterday? I mean *(quarterback)* is phenomenal! Over three hundred yards passing.

BILL

I missed it.

JERRY

MISSED IT! *(Receiver)* made this *miracle* play in the end zone. *(Quarterback)* dropped it right between two of the defense and *(Receiver)* pulled it out of nowhere. What hands! I mean the man is *supernatural*! And (another <u>receiver or running back</u>'s) catching short stuff down the middle time after time. *Amazing*!

BILL

Sounds exciting.

WAITRESS

(Having entered) More coffee, sir?

BILL

Sure, thanks. *(Pours Bill's coffee and exits)*

JERRY

Exciting? It was *life and death!* The lead was back and forth—we pulled it out with less than a minute on the clock. I thought I was gonna die! We have finally got a team. It's the Super Bowl this year for sure!

BILL

Looks good.

JERRY

I'm just glad that Pastor Chambers lets us out by twelve. I mean, I almost missed the pregame show.

WAITRESS

(Finally able to get a word in) More for you, sir?

JERRY

Thank you. *(She fills Jerry's cup and exits.)*

BILL

What'd you think of Chambers' sermon yesterday?

JERRY

(Suddenly, his energy changes.) Uh . . . not bad.

BILL

He has a way of making the truth of Scripture really clear, don't you think?

JERRY

Uh, yeah.

BILL

(Becoming more excited) I'd never really seen the full importance or magnitude of the resurrection before. How central it is to our entire faith! I mean, here are the disciples, defeated and confused. They think the game's up—all is lost. *(The waitress enters with their food.)* Then, WOW! He's alive!

JERRY

Hey, Bill *(Embarrassed)* . . . the waitress.

WAITRESS

Here you go. *(She places their meals before them).*

BILL

Thank you. Anyway, that's an amazing victory! I'm really beginning to see that's where our hope lies!

JERRY

(Whispering) Hold it down.

WAITRESS

Enjoy your breakfast. *(She exits.)*

BILL

(Quieter) I mean the *power* of that is exciting!

JERRY

Yeah, well . . . ah, sure. But no need to get so excited about it right here. Hey, our breakfast is gonna get cold. Shall we . . . ah—*(rubbing his eyebrows as if he's trying to hide)*

BILL

Scratch our eyebrows?

JERRY

(Whispered) Uh, *pray?*

BILL

Yeah.

6

Is It More Blessed to Give Than to Receive?

by
Carol Henegar

THEME: Misusing the body of Christ for our own gain.

RUNNING TIME: Five minutes

CAST:

Ray: owner of a newly opened auto parts store
Dave: a "friendly" customer

PRODUCTION SUGGESTIONS:

Set:
   Should minimally suggest an auto parts store—perhaps a counter with a telephone, calculator, and boxes stacked up behind it.

Props:
   Wallet for Dave
   Box for a car starter
   Calculator
   Large notebook representing an auto parts book

Another option is to mime all set pieces and props.

Is It More Blessed to Give Than to Receive?
THE SCRIPT

(*Ray is in the back room and Dave enters the scene grumbling and exasperated about his car not starting*)

DAVE

(*Talking to himself as he waits for the salesperson*) This is great. Just great. Perfect timing! Why does this always happen to me? Am I blessed, or what? Last week I invest in four new tires and a battery and this week the starter decides to short out on me—probably will cost me an arm and a leg! Am I lucky, or what? Well, this auto parts store better have exactly what I want, or else—

RAY

(*Coming in from the back room*) Hello, may I help you?

DAVE

Oh, what do you know, you're open.

RAY

Sorry, I'm the only one here. I—

DAVE

Yea, it's rough everywhere. Listen, I need a new starter for my car—my old one just died.

RAY

What type of starter do you need?

DAVE

One for a Toy.

RAY

Excuse me?

DAVE

Toyota.

RAY

Oh, right. Which year and model?

DAVE

An '82 Tercel—and I don't have all day.

RAY

Well, I think I can help you out. (*Looking through a parts book*)

DAVE

Hey, you know, you look familiar. I know you from somewhere— (*beginning to warm up*) I got it! You go to my church, don't you? Fifth Avenue Christian?

RAY

Yes, that's my church.

DAVE

So you're "one of us," huh?

RAY

Well, if you mean, am I a Christian? Yes.

DAVE

All right! Hey, brother! (*Reaching out to shake hands*) The name's David Benson. But you can call me Dave.

RAY

Ray, Ray Swanson.

DAVE

Well, hey, Ray, why don't you have a fish or something in your window so people will know you're a Christian. I'd bet you'd get more business.

RAY

Well—

DAVE

Hey, are you in the Yellow Pages?

RAY

Well, yeah—

DAVE

You should put a fish right next to your ad! Pays to advertise!

RAY

Yeah, well . . . (*hands Dave the starter box*) Here's your starter. It comes with a two-year guarantee.
(*Ray figures the price on the calculator*)

DAVE

(*Pulling out his wallet*) Well, I'm ready to break the bank. How much?

RAY

That'll be $89.95.

DAVE

Ninety bucks?!

RAY

That includes tax.

DAVE

Whoa! Hey listen, (*Getting an idea*) Ya know, since we're in the "family" so to speak, why not give me a discount—say, oh, ten bucks off?

RAY

I don't think I can do that.

DAVE

What do you mean you can't do that. Being a Christian means helping each other out, right? Giving that little bit extra to help out a brother in the Lord.

RAY

Well, maybe you're right.

DAVE

Sure, I'm right.

RAY

Do you really believe what you just said?

DAVE

You bet I do!

RAY

Then how about paying $100 for the starter? Just ten bucks more. You see, I just opened this store. I've sunk every dime I have into it. Frankly the profit margin is very small and I'm having a hard time making ends meet. So I thought you might help me out . . . as a brother in the Lord?

                              DAVE

Well, uh . . . that's not exactly what I meant.

                              RAY

Yeah. I know. That will be $89.95.

                              DAVE

Including tax. (*Giving Ray the money*)

                              RAY

Yea, including tax. (*Beginning to make change*) That's $89.95 out of $90.00.

                              DAVE

(*Taking his starter*) Uh, keep the change. (*Dave exits*)

7

Dave and Bruce
by Wayne Harrell

THEME: The folly of comparing ourselves to others.

RUNNING TIME: Five minutes

CAST:

Bruce: quiet, clean-shaven
Dave: bright personality with beard or moustache

PRODUCTION SUGGESTIONS:

Props:
   Two cans of shaving cream
   Two shavers
   Two towels
   Two combs
   Two small tables (suggesting a bathroom counter)
   Box of tissues

Costumes:
   Both characters are dressed in bathrobes and pajama bottoms

Sound:
   Two different alarm clocks ringing
   Two doors slamming

Dave and Bruce
THE SCRIPT

(Offstage two different alarms ring loudly, followed by two doors slamming loudly on either side. DAVE and BRUCE enter from opposite sides of the room groaning and wearing their "morning faces" and drying their hair, as if they just came out of the shower. They stop on opposite sides of the stage area facing the audience. They look into imaginary mirrors in front of them. Neither one is aware of the other.)

BRUCE

Oooooh, Brucey-Brucey-Bruce. What a sight!

DAVE

Oooooh, Dave-O! Why can't we just skip this morning?

BRUCE

That was the longest, most incredible wedding reception I have ever been to.

DAVE

I have never seen so much food.

BRUCE

Ham, meatballs, roast beef—

DAVE

Those weird little quiche things—

BRUCE

Chicken wings, shish-kabob—

DAVE

And the cake—

DAVE AND BRUCE

Ahhhhh, the cake! (*As they squirt shaving cream into their hands with flair*)

BRUCE

Barb and Kevin looked real happy.

DAVE AND BRUCE

And the bridesmaids—*(Slapping the shaving cream on their faces)*

DAVE

Incredible!

BRUCE

Seven bridesmaids—

DAVE AND BRUCE

YOW!

BRUCE

Yeah, *(Sarcastic)* and I sure wowed them, huh? "Hi ya, I'm Bruce. Nice dress." Made a great impression! Boy, am I a jerk! *(Starting to shave)*

DAVE

Old Bruce sure made an impression on the ladies last night. *(Starting to shave)* He's always so attentive: filling glasses, clearing plates, staying late to help clean up.

BRUCE

As usual, Dave was the hit with the women—the smooth style, the easy conversation. He always knows just what to say.

DAVE AND BRUCE

You know, he sure has got it made. He's so—

DAVE

Responsible.

BRUCE

Carefree.

DAVE AND BRUCE

And good looking. And then there's me. *(Making a face in the mirror)*

DAVE

I wear this beard *(moustache)* just to hide my face. If people ever saw what was really behind all this—

BRUCE

Look at this face! You could play "Connect the Dots" on this face. There, right there! A giraffe!

DAVE

Well, I guess I should be thankful I can even grow a beard *(moustache)*.

BRUCE

Lord, isn't there enough ugliness in this world without my face needing to make a contribution?

DAVE

But Bruce, he doesn't have anything to hide.

BRUCE

I wonder if I'd look as good in a beard *(moustache)* as Dave does?

(They both finish shaving and begin to work on their hair.)

DAVE

He's got that full head of hair.

BRUCE

(Combing through his hair) I wonder how much we receded last night?

DAVE

He is so suave and sophisticated.

BRUCE

(Blowing his nose with a loud honk)

DAVE

He's got class.

BRUCE

I am such a wimp.

DAVE

He could date any girl he wanted.

BRUCE

Dave's in perfect shape. *(Putting his contacts in)*

DAVE

(Pinching his waistline) I am so flabby.

BRUCE

Never diets.

DAVE

I've got to go on a diet.

BRUCE

Mr. Charm, that's Dave.

DAVE

Mr. Perfect, that's Bruce.

DAVE AND BRUCE

Ya know, God, if you really loved me, you would have made me just like him. *(Thumbs point to each other and they exit grumbling to themselves)*

Story Theater

8

David and Goliath

by
Kerry Cederberg Meads

THEME: If God is for us, who can be against us?

RUNNING TIME: Ten minutes

CAST:

Charlie: just your Joe Average kind-of-guy
Debbie: bright, energetic, and somewhat childlike
Carol: a bit stuffy, the intellectual
Dan: nice looking, fashion conscious, but casual kind-of-guy

PRODUCTION SUGGESTIONS:

Props:
    Two armless chairs, strong enough to stand on
    Bible

David and Goliath
THE SCRIPT

(The two chairs are set facing the audience about six feet apart.)

CHARLIE

(Enters with his Bible in hand and sits on one of the chairs with a big sigh. He is clearly depressed. He opens his Bible and starts to read.)

"If God be for us, who can be against us?"

(Looks up and sighs and reads again)

"Who can separate us from the love of God?"

(Looks up and sighs and reads again)

"For we are more than conquerors through him that loved us."

(Closes his Bible and sets it on the floor next to him and gives one last big sigh, as his friends Debbie, Dan, and Carol come down the aisle to greet him.)

DEBBIE

(Comes bouncing down the aisle) Hey Charlie—old buddy, old pal!

(Charlie gives a meager wave)

DAN

What's happening? How's it going? *(Charlie shrugs his shoulders.)*

CAROL

Well, obviously, he's depressed.

DEBBIE

What's wrong?

CHARLIE

Life.

CAROL

If I've told you once, I've told you a thousand times. Wake up **and** smell the coffee. Life is hard. Just face it.

DAN

Just ignore it.

DEBBIE

Let's go out for a hot fudge sundae? No guilt, I promise!

CHARLIE

I don't feel like it.

DEBBIE

(Feeling his forehead) Are you sick?

CHARLIE

No.

DAN

Come on, what's wrong?

CHARLIE

Same old thing.

DEBBIE

Ah, the "victorious Christian life" got you down again, huh?

DAN

Just don't think about it. It'll go away.

CAROL

Now wait a minute. Let's deal with this. You're not the only one who's ever felt these things. Why, in each one of us there's an ongoing struggle—a perpetual fight!

DEBBIE

(Standing on the other chair)
A continuing battle—

CHARLIE

A full-scale war—

CAROL

Exactly!

DAN

Speak for yourself!

DEBBIE

There are giants that need to be cut down to size.
(Jumps off the chair)

CAROL

Completely slain!

CHARLIE

But, how do I do it?

CAROL

Very astute question.

DEBBIE

Well, God gives us a perfect example. *(She goes to get Charlie's Bible.)*

DAN

Perfect, did I hear the word "perfect"?

DEBBIE

In David.

CHARLIE

David?

DEBBIE

As in David and Goliath. *(Giving him his Bible)*

CHARLIE

Oh sure, David and Goliath. It's easy to talk about overcoming giants when they're miles away. But what do you do when they're camping in your own backyard?

DAN

They can't. You live in an apartment. *(Dan and Carol laugh.)*

CAROL

Besides if you're looking for a role model, maybe you shouldn't set your sights so high. Why not start a little lower . . . with someone like Zacchaeus. *(Dan and Carol laugh again)*

DEBBIE
Wait a minute. David is a great role model. God is no respecter of persons. God is well pleased to make us unique and different for his own purpose.

CAROL

Yes, well, all I've got to say is God had a lot more to work with in David.

CHARLIE

Excuse me?

CAROL

(Taking the Bible from Charlie)
He killed a lion and a bear with his bare hands.

DAN

Whoa! Talk about physically fit. *(Charlie looks down at himself.)*

CAROL

And listen to this. *(Reading the Bible)* "Behold, I have seen a son of Jesse the Bethlehemite who is a skillful musician, a mighty man of valor, a warrior, one prudent in speech . . . and a handsome man."

DAN

He sure had a lot going for him. *(Charlie becomes more depressed.)*

CAROL

(Continues reading) "He was ruddy, with beautiful eyes and a handsome appearance." *(Closing Bible)* I mean when you compare this *(Pointing at Charlie)* to David—

CHARLIE

(Sitting) There's no comparison.

CAROL

"So as a man thinks of himself, so he is."

DEBBIE

(Retorting) But, "God sees not as a man sees, for man looks at the outward appearance, but the Lord looks at the heart."

CHARLIE

I'd rather be handsome.

DEBBIE

Wait, wait, wait. *(Taking Charlie's Bible and standing on the chair, she gives the Bible to Charlie and points to the story of David and Goliath.)* The God who is at work in your life is the same God that worked in David—the same giant killer!

(Debbie grabs Dan and pulls him to one side. Charlie grabs Carol and takes her over to his side.)

DEBBIE

"Now the Philistines gathered their armies for battle. They stood on the mountain on one side." *(Debbie stands on a chair to represent the Philistines.)*

CHARLIE

(Now inspired) "While Israel stood on the mountain on the other side *(Charlie stands on his chair to represent the Israelites)* , with the valley between them." *(Everyone looks down into the space between the chairs.)*

ALL

(Gasp) Ooh!

CHARLIE

(Coming down from the chair) Then a champion came out from the armies of the Philistines named Goliath.

(Debbie sits Dan in the chair and proceeds to climb on his shoulders so they can become Goliath.)

DAN

Careful, careful.

DEBBIE

Sorry!

David and Goliath /67

CAROL

I have a feeling you're going to look foolish.

DAN

Perish the thought.

CHARLIE

"His height was six cubits and a span." (*Dan stands with Debbie on his shoulders.*)

CAROL

Approximately nine feet nine inches.

CHARLIE

"And he had a bronze helmet on his head and was clothed with scale-armor which weighed 5000 shekels of bronze."

CAROL

Which comes to about 1250 pounds.
(*Dan collapses onto the chair with a gasp.*)

CHARLIE

"He also had bronze greaves."

DEBBIE & DAN

(*Looking at Charlie*) Bronze greaves?

CAROL

Shin guards.

CHARLIE

"And a bronze javelin slung between his shoulders. And the shaft of his spear was like a weaver's beam (*Debbie holds an imaginary spear*) and the head of his spear weighed 600 shekels of iron."

CAROL

Which comes to—

DAN

All right, so Goliath was no lightweight. I think they've got the point.

CHARLIE

"Goliath stood. . . . *(Dan doesn't move.)* Goliath stood! *(Dan stands.)* "And shouted to the ranks of Israel. . . ."

DEBBIE

(In her best macho voice) Yo! Israel! "Choose a man for yourselves and let him come down to me."

CHARLIE

"And the Philistine came forward *(Dan takes a step forward)* morning and evening for forty days and took his stand."

DEBBIE

(Bouncing up and down on Dan's shoulders) Monday, Tuesday, Wednesday, Thurs—

DAN

(Stopping her) This is getting to be a bit much. *(Sits down again)*

CHARLIE

(Handing the Bible to Carol and taking a step forward, as he becomes the character of David) Now David arose early in the morning and came to the camp of Israel and David entered in order to greet his brothers. As he was talking to them, behold, the champion the Philistine was coming up from the army of the Philistines *(Dan comes forward again)*, and he spoke the same words. *(Debbie starts to speak.)*

DEBBIE

"Choose a man—"

David and Goliath /69

CAROL

I think we all remember them.

CHARLIE

And David heard them and said to Saul *(Kneeling before Carol pretending she is Saul)*, "Let no man's heart fail him. I, your servant will go and fight the Philistine."

CAROL

I see. Well, don't forget to pack a lunch.

CHARLIE

(Mimes the following action) And he took his sling in his hand and chose for himself five smooth stones from the brook. And he approached the Philistine and the Philistine said to David—

DEBBIE

"Am I a dog that you come to me with sticks?" *(Laughs)*

CHARLIE

Then it happened when the Philistine arose *(Dan rises)* and came and drew near to meet David *(Dan steps forward)*, that David ran quickly toward the battle line.

(Miming the following action) And David put his hand into his bag and took from it a stone and slung it. And it struck the Philistine on his forehead, so that he fell on his face to the ground. *(Dan eases Debbie's feet to the floor so she can fall safely.)*

DAN

(Sitting again) Whew! What a relief.

CHARLIE

(Again miming the following action) Then David ran and stood over the Philistine and took his sword and drew it out of its sheath and killed him.

(Debbie does a spectacular death scene.)

And from that day on, David went out wherever Saul sent him, and he prospered!

EVERYONE

(Cheering) Yeah!

DAN

That's what I like to hear!

CAROL

"V" for victory.

CHARLIE

I can't believe it. It's so easy to forget—the God that gave David victory over Goliath is the same God that is at work in my life.

DEBBIE

He who has begun a good work in you will bring it to completion on the day of our Lord Jesus Christ.

CHARLIE

(Reading his Bible) "For I am persuaded, that neither death, nor life, nor angels, nor principalities, nor powers, nor things present, nor things to come, nor height, nor depth, nor any other creature, shall be able to separate us from the love of God, which is in Christ Jesus our Lord." *(They all run off.)*

9

The Three Little Pigs and the Architect

by Judy Urschel

THEME: The foolish man builds his house upon the sand, but the wise man builds his house upon the rock.

RUNNING TIME: Eight minutes

CAST:

Narrator/Architect
Pig 1: a party animal
Pig 2: a corporate executive
Pig 3: a weekend handyman

PRODUCTION SUGGESTIONS:

Props:
    Bible
    Pig 1: table loaded with chips and sodas, racquetball and ping-pong paddles, etc.
    Pig 2: desk with phone, coffee mug, and several very organized piles of paperwork
    Pig 3: several piles of two-by-fours, a carpenter's apron and a tape measure

Costumes:
    Narrator/Architect: regular street clothes,
    Pig 1: dressed for a beach party (shorts, Hawaiian shirt, sun glasses, etc.)
    Pig 2: suit and tie
    Pig 3: overalls and flannel shirt, hat

The Three Little Pigs and the Architect
THE SCRIPT

(The three little pigs each have an area of the stage that is their own space representing their "house." Their backs are toward the audience.)

NARRATOR

(Reading his Bible to the audience) And Jesus said, "Everyone who hears these words of mine and does not put them into practice is like a foolish man who built his house on sand. The rains came, the floods rose, the winds blew and beat against that house, and it fell, and great was the fall of it."

Once upon a time, there were three little pigs.

PIG 1

(Turning around) Let's party! *(Freeze action)*

PIG 2

(Turning around and picking up the phone) Miss Hardwick, hold all my calls and cancel all my appointments. *(Freeze action)*

PIG 3

(Turning around, trying to measure an imaginary window) I think thirty-eight inches by . . . well, maybe thirty-four by . . . well, maybe over here is better. *(Freeze action)*

NARRATOR

Although the three little pigs were very different from one another, they did have one thing in common. They were all designing their own house. One day, the first little pig was visited by a stranger. *(Narrator indicates himself)*

PIG 1

(As Pig 1 speaks, Pigs 2 and 3 turn their backs to the audience.)
Hey! Come on in! Welcome to the party! Just make yourself at home. Food and drinks are in here, the video games and wide-screen TV are in the den, racquetball court's downstairs, and there's ping-pong out on the deck.

ARCHITECT

This is quite a place you have here.

PIG 1

Believe it! Built it myself—designed the whole thing, too. Think it's the beach house to end all beach houses.

ARCHITECT

Oh, you've got a volleyball net set up out there, too.

PIG 1

Of course! Can't live on a beach and not play volleyball. We'll get a game going later. I've also got equipment for windsurfing, parasailing, skiing, and scuba diving. So, big guy, just let me know. What's your pleasure.

ARCHITECT

It sounds like lots of fun, but—

PIG 1

Well, hey, isn't that what life's all about? The one with the most toys wins! Hey, I'm not sure if I've met you before. You must be a friend of a friend or something like that.

ARCHITECT

Well, actually I—

PIG 1

Hey look, I don't care! I'll tell you straight. This is my place. It's set up just the way I like it. If you want to be where the fun is, stick with me. I'll show you how to have a good time.

ARCHITECT

Does that include the house falling down?

PIG 1

(Laughing) The house falling down? That's a good one! You planning on skydiving through my roof or something?

ARCHITECT

No, I'm telling you your house is going to fall down.

PIG 1

What's the joke?

ARCHITECT

I'm an architect. I came in to talk to you because I saw that your house was built on sand. There's no foundation and the walls are beginning to cave-in. You see, your house is built out of straw.

PIG 1

Straw? Oh, come on. Sure, I'll admit that brickwork by the fireplace is actually plastic molding. And those beams up there? Prefab Styrofoam, but who cares? It looks good, so why bother with the expense of the real thing?

ARCHITECT

But one big storm and the whole thing comes down.

PIG 1

Look, I told you, I designed and built this house *myself*. For *me*. The way I like it. And it's great! I can do exactly as I please, whenever *I* want to.

ARCHITECT

But I—

PIG 1

Hey, buddy, I don't mind having people around to share my good times, but I don't like people who put a damper on things. Maybe you should just leave.

ARCHITECT

I'd really like to help—

PIG 1

The only help I want is to have a good time. Work on thinking a little more positive, then you can come back. I just don't want a "Gloomy Gus" hanging around, you know what I mean? Adios! *(Turns back to the audience and freezes all action)*

NARRATOR

Well, the next day the stranger happened to drop by to see the second little pig at his house.

PIG 2

(Turning around and putting his feet up on his desk) My secretary says you were very insistent about making an appointment to see me.

ARCHITECT

Yes, I have some important information—

PIG 2

What company?

ARCHITECT

No, you don't understand. I'm an architect and a builder and—

PIG 2

Architects are a dime a dozen. I employed hundreds of them to build this. You realize, of course, that you are sitting in the most state-of-the-art office building in the country? It's the corporate headquarters for five multi-national corporations, sixteen manufacturing conglomerates, a score of—

ARCHITECT

Yes. I know all that, but I came to tell you that your building won't last.

PIG 2

Ha! This building has the most advanced design—

ARCHITECT

But it's on a fault line. One tremor and the whole thing will crumble.

PIG 2

Look, this happens to be the prime location of the city. And this building will withstand anything.

ARCHITECT

But it's built out of twigs.

PIG 2

Twigs. Interesting sense of humor you have. I'll have you know this is genuine, first-cut cedar imported from the Canadian coastal range.

ARCHITECT

You need to start all over—on a solid foundation with—

PIG 2

I'm very happy with this the way it is, but my company *is* looking into building some new factories down in South America. If you want to put in a bid you can get the information from my secretary, Miss Hardwick, on your way out.

ARCHITECT

I'm sorry, I only design for people, not companies. I'd like to design a home for you.

PIG 2

Well, then you really are wasting my time. This *is* my home. Who I am and what I am are all right here. Thank you very much for your "appraisal" and good-day. *(Turns back to audience and freezes action)*

NARRATOR

Well, the following day the stranger stopped by the third little pig's—*(Seeing the pile of wood)* Uh—

PIG 3

(Turning around measuring a board with his tape measure) Oh, I don't know . . . maybe if I . . . then again . . .

NARRATOR

The stranger stopped by the third little pig's construction site.

PIG 3

Oh, that'll never work.

ARCHITECT

Excuse me, but what are you building?

PIG 3

You know, that's a good question. I keep starting different designs, but I'm never quite able to finish them quite the way I'd like to. I started building over there *(Pointing out toward the audience)*, and the thing sank.

ARCHITECT

I'm not surprised. That's a swamp.

PIG 3

Why, so it is! I never noticed that. Sure noticed the mosquitoes, though. Well, anyway, I just thought I'd try building right on this mountainside—pretty view and all that. What do you think of that?

ARCHITECT

I hate to say this, but the first time it rained, your house would slide away.

PIG 3

You know, you're right! I never would have thought of that. How come you know so much?

ARCHITECT

I'm an architect.

PIG 3

Well, isn't this a great piece of luck! Boy, your help could sure come in handy. Now if you'd just grab a couple of those two-by-fours, there was a nice little place just down the road that I passed by this morning that I liked the style of—

ARCHITECT

I'm afraid I don't work like that.

PIG 3

Well, I don't mind carrying everything.

ARCHITECT

No, that's not what I mean.

PIG 3

Can't give away the secrets of your trade, huh?

ARCHITECT

It's nothing like that.

PIG 3

I understand. You probably have lots better things to do than mess around with a little guy like me. Guess I was presuming too much.

ARCHITECT

Oh no, I want to help you.

PIG 3

But I thought you just said—

ARCHITECT

It's just that when I work on a project, I have to be the only architect. It just won't work any other way.

PIG 3

Wait a second. You're telling me that you want to design my house?

ARCHITECT

Yes.

PIG 3

Well, what's your fee?

ARCHITECT

No charge. Just give me control of the design.

PIG 3

But what about my own ideas and taste?

ARCHITECT

Don't worry, I'll take your personality into account. I happen to know you quite well. But I'm concerned that your foundation is solid and that the building materials are of the highest quality.

PIG 3

You could leave a set of instructions.

ARCHITECT

Oh, you'll have great blueprints and I'll be working right beside you.

PIG 3

This is amazing! I admit I haven't been that great at picking out places. Why kid myself? I'm no architect or builder. You've got yourself a deal! *(They shake on it.)* Come on, I'll buy you a cup of coffee. *(Pig 3 turns around and freezes action)*

NARRATOR

(Reading out of his Bible to the audience) And Jesus said, "Everyone who hears these words of mine and puts them into practice is like a wise man who built his house on the rock. The rains came, the floods rose, and the winds blew and beat against that house, but it did not fall, because it had been built on the rock."

10

The Farmer, the Soldier, and the Prisoner

by Deborah Gilmour Smyth

THEME: God's call to his service

RUNNING TIME: Eight minutes

CAST:

Narrator: a pleasant and expressive voice
Farmer: a friendly, agreeable fellow, more casual physically
Soldier: strong, military-like in speech and behavior
Prisoner: haggard, bitter, mocking, without hope
King: caring, authoritative, Christ-like

PRODUCTION SUGGESTIONS:

Props:
    One to three stools or chairs for Farmer, Soldier, and Prisoner

Costumes:
    Farmer: perhaps jeans and a flannel shirt
    Soldier: khaki or camouflage pants and a tan shirt, a sense of a uniform
    Prisoner: disheveled, plain T-shirt and dark pants, barefoot
    King: casual street clothes,
    Narrator: pleasant dress

Style:
   Presented like a fairy tale—just a bit bigger than life, but sharp and focused.

   The movement should be simple and economical.

If you have a very short rehearsal period, this piece will work well as Reader's Theater. (Reader's Theater is discussed in greater detail in Lamb's Players Present Developing a Drama Group, published by World Wide Publications.)

The Farmer, the Soldier, and the Prisoner
THE SCRIPT

(The actors enter and remain still with their backs and sides to audience until the Narrator introduces each one.)

NARRATOR

Once upon a time, in a faraway land, there was a king who dearly loved his subjects. *(King turns toward audience)* And in this land were many people with different customs and different languages. Now and then, the king would issue a special gift to some of his people—a call. A call to become one of the king's messengers.

Now in the king's land lived a farmer. *(Farmer turns out and demonstrates the following with one or two subtle movements)* His life was simple and disciplined. He plowed his fields, tended the soil, harvested the crops, and fed his family. He loved the king and was happy. One day the farmer went out to survey his crops. As he stood looking out over his fields, he noticed suddenly that someone stood beside him.

(The farmer and the king stand side-by-side looking out.)

KING

Good farmer, what do you see?

FARMER

I see the abundance of my fields and my heart is glad, for my family will want for nothing.

NARRATOR

And then the Stranger touched the farmer and his eyes were opened. He turned, and for the first time, recognized the face of his king.

FARMER

My Lord—

NARRATOR

The farmer knelt down but the King lifted him up and said—

KING

Look again, my friend. What do you see?

NARRATOR

The farmer looked and saw—

FARMER

I see the lands beyond my own gate—with men, women, and children in need. I see loneliness and fear and pain, people hungry in body and soul.

NARRATOR

Then the king touched the farmer and the farmer's heart was broken.

FARMER

My Lord, what can I do for these?

KING

Good farmer, I call you to be my messenger to the poor, my helper to the needy. To comfort those who mourn, and proclaim the good news of my deliverance.

(Farmer turns away from the audience)

NARRATOR

Now in another part of that land there lived a soldier—a young and willing servant in the army of the king. As the soldier stood surveying the field of a coming battle, he sensed that someone stood beside him. For some time the stranger did not speak, but gazed out at the field.

KING

Good soldier, what do you see?

SOLDIER

I see the field of a great battle.

KING

Do you see victory?

SOLDIER

I see neither victory nor defeat, I only know that I must fight.

NARRATOR

Then the stranger touched the soldier and his ears were opened, and he knew the sound of his commander's voice.

SOLDIER

My king—

NARRATOR

As the soldier began to kneel, the king lifted him up and said—

KING

Good soldier, tell me, what do you hear?

NARRATOR

And the soldier listened.

SOLDIER

I hear the sound of distant thunder, a trumpet call proclaiming a great day of judgment that none shall escape.

NARRATOR

And the king touched the soldier and the soldier's heart was broken.

SOLDIER

My captain, what are your orders?

KING

I am calling you to be a messenger in the army of the king, to proclaim a warning of the coming judgment.

(Soldier turns away from the audience)

NARRATOR

Now the last man in our story did not serve the king. He was arrogant and boastful—an outcast in the land. He had lived his life as an enemy of the king. And now he was a prisoner of his own crimes, condemned to death. He lay bound in chains—wretched, bitter, weeping. One moment he would raise his fist in anger, and the next moment, sink into hopeless despair. One day as he cried out his rage he saw a stranger standing in the corner of his cell. The stranger did not speak, but there was a passion in his silence. The prisoner felt a chill—like a piercing wind—run through his soul.

PRISONER

Are you my executioner? *(Bitterly)*

KING

I am the Life.

PRISONER

Life. *(With irony)* My soul gasps for life, but I am dying in this pit and there is none to save me. My chains hold fast, there is no hope. Only death will come.

NARRATOR

Then the stranger touched the prisoner and his eyes were opened. He looked up into the face of the stranger and saw an overwhelming love—a love that burned. For the first time in his life he saw his own need—and he understood. He saw his king.

PRISONER

Please don't look on me—I am too dirty, too vile. You are truth and light. My life has been only lies and darkness. I deserve these chains. I deserve this death.

NARRATOR

But the king reached down and lifted the prisoner up. His chains fell off and his wounds were healed.

KING

My friend, you are a free man.

PRISONER

My lord, I am not deserving of this love. Please tell me how I can repay this gift—

KING

The payment has already been made. *(King reaches to the prisoner with outstretched hand—as though to take his hand)*

NARRATOR

And then the prisoner saw the nail prints in the king's hands, and his heart was broken.

PRISONER

My lord, let me be your servant.

KING

I am calling you to be my messenger to those who are bound in sin and death—to proclaim to them the freedom I have given you.

PRISONER

(Turning out to audience) The Spirit of the Lord is on me—

FARMER

(Turning out to audience) He has called me—

SOLDIER

(Turning out to audience) He has sent me—

FARMER

To preach the good news to the poor.

SOLDIER

To proclaim the coming judgment of our God.

PRISONER

To proclaim freedom for the captive and release for the prisoner.

FARMER

He has opened my eyes—

SOLDIER

(Building) He has unstopped my ears—

PRISONER

He has released me from the bondage of sin—

ALL

(Simply, gently) He has broken my heart—

NARRATOR

(With finality) To preach to the nations, the gospel of his salvation.

11

The Parable of the Assignments

by Deborah Gilmour Smyth

THEME: God's call, the stumbling blocks, and the help and comfort of the Holy Spirit.

RUNNING TIME: Eight to ten minutes

CAST:

Narrator: pleasant voice and storytelling style
Servant 1: a joyful and carefree countenance
Servant 2: confident, a deliberate and studied presence
Servant 3: defeated and afraid
Counselor (female): this character represents the Holy Spirit
Truth-Twister: represents the evil one, movement should be more wild and erratic.

All but the Narrator should be comfortable and skilled in movement or dance. If you have someone who is familiar with any fluid style of martial arts, try casting them as Counselor (contrasting that kind of movement against the wilder, more erratic movement of Truth Twister). Counselor alternates between the strong martial art movement directed toward Truth-Twister and the more gentle, comforting movement directed toward Servants.

PRODUCTION SUGGESTIONS:

Props:
   One ladder: you might use this for Narrator and Counselor to watch the action so that the major portion of the stage is left for movement
   Three backpacks that can be attached to each of the servants

Style:
This piece works best if you have performers who are comfortable expressing themselves through movement or dance. Although the movement *can* be very simple, skilled choreography enhances the presentation.

Note:
Narrator's lines could be divided into a Reader's Theater format, however, we found that the visual, non-verbal approach to characters of Servants, Counselor, and Truth Twister to be very effective

The Parable of the Assignments
THE SCRIPT

SERVANT 1

Serve the Lord!

SERVANT 2

Serve the Lord!

SERVANT 3

Serve the Lord!

COUNSELOR

With gladness.

NARRATOR

and now—

ALL

(Shout) THE PARABLE OF THE ASSIGNMENTS

(All but Narrator turn away from audience)

NARRATOR

Once upon a time, not so very long ago, in a place very much like this, there were three servants. They weren't particularly well known and they didn't possess unusual brilliance or outstanding abilities. But they were servants of a great and mighty king.

The king loved his servants. He called them by name, called them friends, and honored them by giving them each a task to carry out, a goal to reach, and the path to follow. The king sent to his servants a counselor *(Counselor turns to face audience)* that would help them on their way-by guiding and comforting them, and by encouraging them and bringing them joy.

(Counselor helps each servant with their backpacks)

Now, it happened that each servant was given an assignment and sent on a journey to another land. The counselor of the servants fastened their loads and set them upon their paths, with the king's admonition:

(Here counselor may use dance, martial art, or abstract images with mime to communicate to the servants.)

"You are my ambassadors and have been given a trust and a path to follow. The road may prove rough and the way hard. And be aware, there is one who wants to deceive you and divert you from your path and cause you to cast away the assignments you have been given. His appearance seems friendly, but his name is Truth Twister and he is a fearsome enemy. Do not entertain him with argument for he is a master of deceit. He will convince you that black is white and day is night. Hold fast to the assignment you've been given and do not be afraid. Your load is not too heavy, and help will come when it is needed."

NARRATOR

(Servant 1 is the focus) `And then, the first step. One servant began with eagerness—running and leaping—his work being joy for the master's sake. But, as he ran, he became lonely and began to slow his pace—longing for a companion to run and play with him. The longing became a heaviness in his heart. Suddenly *(Truth-Twister enters, perhaps from a previously hidden place)*, a bright creature ran beside him—playing, laughing, calling out,

(Perhaps use games of leap frog or tag that turn into pushes and shoves.)

"Come, run with me. This way! The path you run on leads to nothing. I know the way to adventure. You will have many companions—many friends who will run and play with you. Come, run with me."

The voice of the stranger was strangely sweet and the servant was tired of running alone, so he followed the stranger. They laughed and played, gamboled and leaped. But the stranger grew rough and his laughter grew sinister and frightening. He pushed and shoved and tripped the servant causing him to fall hard to the ground. The servant cowered in fear for his life.

(Counselor intervenes and defeats Truth Twister. You might use the same series of movements each time this happens.)

But as the king had promised, the counselor came and Truth-Twister was defeated and fled in anger.

(Truth Twister retreats but is still seen—perhaps crouched and waiting. Servant 1 is comforted by Counselor and goes into a neutral position until the end)

(Servant 2 comes into focus) The next servant began with confidence. Calculating each step—every move deliberate. He was in control. *(Truth-Twister moves in subtly)* In time, the path became rocky and the air was hot and heavy. He became more weary with each step. His thirst was unbearable. Suddenly, he saw a stream. Its waters looked cool and refreshing. It seemed to call to him:

(Soothing) "Come. Look. Drink."

Leaning over the fragrant waters, he was captivated by his own reflection. He was very pleased with what he saw. Again the liquid voice called:

"Come, look. What a beautiful creature you are. You possess greatness. Why, you could be king!"

The voice was mesmerizing and the servant leaned further and further over the waters. Suddenly, he slipped from the rocky bank into his own icy reflection. The stream became a torrent of angry, laughing water. He thought he would drown.
(Again Counselor intervenes. There is a battle with Truth Twister for Servant 2)

But the counselor came and Truth Twister was defeated.

(Servant 2 goes to a neutral position until the end.)

*(Servant 3 is in focus.)*The last servant was very much afraid *(Truth Twister moves in)* of the task he had been given. He could not

even take the first step. A voice within said,

"It is certain you will fail. The task is too hard. You will never complete it. Why even try. You can't do it. The King demands too much."

The voice chattered on and on until the servant's own lips began repeating,

I *can't* do it. The task *is* too hard. The King demands too much. I *will* fail.

(Counselor moves in)

And the servant sat down and wept. That is where the counselor found him - weeping and angry—not willing to go on. The counselor offered comfort and implored the servant to stand firm and hold fast to his call. "Help is here and Truth Twister is defeated." But the servant only wept and moaned:

SERVANT 3

"I will fail . . . . I will fail."

NARRATOR

And there our story ends. We have a choice, for we are ambassadors.

SERVANTS

(All up and out to audience) We are servants to this great and mighty king.

SERVANT 2

(To audience) The Lord has chosen us—

SERVANT 1

To serve him.

SERVANT 2

To trust him.

SERVANT 3

He will not ask more than we can bear.

NARRATOR

For the counselor—

COUNSELOR

the comforter—

NARRATOR AND COUNSELOR

Has come—and is with us.

ALL

Stand firm.

NARRATOR

Let nothing move you.

COUNSELOR

Serve the Lord—

ALL

with gladness!

Choral Readings

12

The Glory of the Lord

compiled by
Kerry Cederberg Meads

THEME: The glory of the gospel

RUNNING TIME: Seven minutes

CAST:

Reader 1 (man)
Reader 2 (woman)
Reader 3 (man)
Reader 4 (woman)
Reader 5 (man)

PRODUCTION SUGGESTIONS:

Props:
    Five uniform black notebooks to hold the scripts

Costumes:
    Coordinated street clothes giving a clean, professional look

The Glory of the Lord
THE SCRIPT

ALL: In the beginning was the Word, and the Word was with God, and the Word was God.

READER 3: He was in the beginning with God.

READER 1: All things came into being by him, and apart from him nothing came into being that has come into being.

READER 2: The heavens

READER 4: The heavens

ALL: The heavens are telling of the glory of God:

READER 5: Their expanse is declaring the work of his hands.

4: Day to day

MEN: Pours forth speech,

3: And night to night

WOMEN: Reveals knowledge.

1: Sing to the Lord,

WOMEN: A new song.

4: Sing to the Lord,

ALL: All the earth.

5: Tell of his glory among all nations.

2: His wonderful deeds among all the peoples.

3: For great is the Lord,

1, 3, 5: And greatly,

ALL: To be praised.

4: He is to be feared above all gods.

WOMEN: For all the gods of the people are idols.

3: But the Lord made the heavens.

2: Splendor

1: And majesty

3: Are before him.

5: All strength

4: And beauty

3: Are his sanctuary.

2: Let the glory of the Lord endure forever;

WOMEN: Let the Lord be glad in his works,

3: He looks at the earth

WOMEN: And it trembles,

MEN: He touches the mountains

WOMEN: And they smoke.

ALL: Give to the Lord,

MEN: The glory of his name,

3: Bring an offering and come into his courts.

1, 2: Worship the Lord in the splendor of

ALL: Holiness.

The Glory of the Lord / 103

4, 5: Tremble before him

ALL: All the earth.

1: The Lord reigns!

2: He is clothed with majesty

3: And has girded himself with strength.

4: Indeed the world is firmly established.

5: It will not be moved.

WOMEN: Thy throne is established from of old.

MEN: Thou art from everlasting

ALL: To everlasting.

(*Pause*)

3: Oh Lord,

WOMEN: Our Lord,

1: How majestic is thy name in all the earth.

5: Who has displayed thy splendors

MEN: Above thy heavens.

2: When I consider thy heavens,

4: The work of thy fingers.

1, 5: The moon and the stars which thou hast ordained. . .

3: What is man that thou dost take thought of him?

WOMEN: And the son of man,

3: That thou dost care for him?

1, 5: God has looked down from the heavens upon the sons of men,

WOMEN: To see if there is anyone who understands,

2: Who seeks after God.

4: Every one of them has turned aside,

1, 2, 4, 5: Together they have become . . .

5: Corrupt. There is no one who does good,

2: Not even me.

4: Be gracious to me, O God,

MEN: According to thy lovingkindness:

WOMEN: According to the greatness of thy compassion,

ALL: Blot out my transgressions.

3: Wash me thoroughly

1, 2: From my iniquity,

3: And cleanse me

4, 5: From my sin.

2: For I know my transgressions,

4: And my sin is ever before me.

ALL: Against thee,

3: Thee only, I have sinned, and done what is evil in thy sight.

MEN: Do return, O Lord,

ALL: How long will it be?

WOMEN: And be sorry for thy servant,

1: Will the Lord reject forever?

5: And will he never be favorable again?

The Glory of the Lord / 105

4: Has his lovingkindness ceased?

2: Has his promise come to an end forever?

3: Has God forgotten to be gracious?

WOMEN: Or has he in anger . . .

4: Withdrawn his compassion?

MEN: Lord, how long

3: How long,

1, 5: Wilt thou look on?

WOMEN: God be gracious to us,

2: And bless us,

4: That thy way may be known on the earth,

2: Thy salvation among all nations.

WOMEN: Bow thy heavens, O Lord,

ALL: And come down.

(*Pause*)

3: And the Word became flesh, and dwelt among us;

ALL: And we beheld his glory.

4: Glory as of the only begotten of the Father,

5: Grace and truth were realized through Jesus Christ.

2: And being found in appearance as a man, he humbled himself by becoming obedient,

1: To the point of death,

3: Even death on a cross.

1, 5: Therefore also God highly exalted him,

WOMEN: And bestowed on him the name which is above every name.

3: That at the name of Jesus every knee should bow, . . .

2, 3, 4: And that every tongue should confess,

ALL: Jesus Christ is Lord.

3: To the glory of God.

2: And he is the radiance of his glory

WOMEN: And the exact representation of his nature,

ALL: And upholds all things by the word of his power.

MEN: And when he had made purification of sins, he sat down at the right hand of the Majesty on high.

WOMEN: Blessed be his glorious name forever!

MEN: Let the earth be filled with his glory!

ALL: Let everything that has breath

WOMEN: Praise

MEN: Praise

ALL: Praise the Lord!

13

Our Weakness, His Strength

by
Kerry Cederberg Meads

THEME: God's promise of strength in our weakness

RUNNING TIME: Five minutes

CAST:

Voice 1 - Lead Vocal
Echo 2
Echo 3
Echo 4

PRODUCTION SUGGESTIONS:

Props:
    A chair

Costume:
    Voice 1: loose-fitting, white or light colored clothing
    Echo 2, 3, 4: loose fitting, black or dark colored clothing

As little attention as possible should be drawn to the costumes so the main focus is on the voices.

Style:
    This particular piece works well when the lines are memorized along with minimal movement. If rehearsal time is prohibitive, it is also very effective as Reader's Theater.

Our Weakness, His Strength
THE SCRIPT

(A chair is center stage and Voice 1 stands directly in front of it. Echoes 2, 3, and 4 stand evenly spaced behind Voice 1.)

Voice 1: Oh Lord, my Lord,

Echo 2: My savior,

Echo 3: My God,

Echo 4: My strength.

Voice 1: You promised—

Echo 2: *(Brightly)* They shall mount up with wings like eagles,

Echo 3: *(Brighter)* They shall run and not grow weary,

Echo 4: *(Even brighter)* They shall walk and not faint,

All: *(Brightest)* You promised!

(Pause)

Voice 1: But, I—

Echo 2,3,4: *(Hushed tone)* I am tired.

Voice 1: And my eyes are failing me. *(Very slowly begins to sink into the chair)*

Echo 2: I trip—

Echo 3: I stumble—

Echo 4: I fall—

Voice 1: Too often, too hard.

Echo 2,3,4: *(Hushed tone)* I am weak—

Voice 1: Too weak. *(Head bowed)*

Echo 2,3,4: *(Lacking energy)* I cannot lift my head.

(Pause)

Voice 1: *(Slowly raising head, gaining strength vocally)* I can do all things . . . through Christ . . . who strengthens me. I can do all things through Christ . . . who strengthens . . . *(Begins to stand slowly)*

Echo 2: *(Energetically)* I want to run for you.

Echo 3: *(Energetically)* To go the distance.

Echo 4: *(Energetically)* You know it is the desire of my heart—

All: To fulfill the call—

Voice 1: *(Standing, looking up)* Your call!

(Pause)

Echo 2: I wonder if I heard you?

Echo 3: Really heard you,

Echo 4: Or if it was just—

Voice 1: *(Stepping out slightly from the chair, as if to stop the voices)* No, it is the desire of my heart to—

Echo 2,3,4: *(Gently)* My heart—

Voice 1: Oh God, my God *(Very slowly sinking to the knees)* I feel broken, bruised. I—

Echo 2: Question,

Echo 2,3: Doubt,

Echo 2,3,4: Fear.

All: I feel low,

Echo 2,3,4: Dispensable,

Echo 2,3: Insignificant,

Voice 1: *(Kneeling next to chair)* Small. I am without inspiration— *(Burying head in arms upon the chair)*

Echo 2: Joy,

Echo 2,3: Hope.

Echo 2,3,4: *(Hushed tone)* I am alone. *(Bowing heads)*

(Pause)

Voice 1: *(Uncovering head)* You promised—

Echo 2: *(Raise head)* That you would never leave me.

Voice 1: You promised—

Echo 3: *(Raise head)* That you would be my comfort.

Echo 4: *(Raise head)* That from the love of God—

Echo 2,3,4: Nothing could separate me.

Echo 2,3: Nothing.

Voice 1: Nothing can separate me—

Echo 2,3,4: *(Gently)* From the love of God.

(Pause)

Voice 1: Melt me. *(Slowly rising to sit on the chair)*

Echo 2,3,4: *(Gently)* Restore me.

Voice 1: You are the lifter of my head.

Echo 2,3,4: My strength, my salvation.

Voice 1: You are the light of my eyes,

Echo 2,3,4: The truth, the way.

Voice 1: *(Gently)* You are the gentle whisper,

Echo 2,3,4: *(Hushed tone)* The still, the small voice.

Voice 1: *(Sitting)* Touch me again, so I might—

Echo 2: Reach out—

Echo 3: And touch my brother,

Echo 4: And see his need

Voice 1: As you have seen mine.

All: Spirit of the Living God,

Echo 2,3,4: *(Hushed tone)* Fall afresh—

Voice 1: *(Standing)* On me.

14

The Lord's Unfailing Love

compiled by
Deborah Gilmour Smyth

THEME: God's unfailing love

RUNNING TIME: Six minutes

CAST:

Reader 1 (woman)
Reader 2 (woman)
Reader 3 (man)
Reader 4 (man)
Reader 5 (man)

PRODUCTION SUGGESTIONS:

Props:
   Five uniform black notebooks to hold the scripts

Costumes:
   Coordinated street clothes giving a clean, professional look

The Lord's Unfailing Love
THE SCRIPT

(Readers stand facing the audience in order: 3, 1, 5, 2, 4)

Readers 1,2: Sing!

Reader 3: Sing praises to God!

Readers 1,2: Sing!

Reader 4: Sing praises to our King!

Readers 1,2: Sing!

Reader 5: Sing praises.

Readers 1,2,3,4: For God is the King of all the earth.

Reader 5: From the lips of children and infants you have ordained praise.

Reader 3: Your love, oh Lord, reaches to the heavens,

1,2: Sing to him a new song!

4: Your faithfulness to the skies—

1,2: Shout for joy!

5: How priceless is your unfailing love.

1,2: Clap your hands all you people!

1,2,4: Sing joyfully to the Lord!

5: Both high and low among men find refuge in—

1,2,5: *(Hushed)* The shadow of your wings.

All: Oh Lord,

2: *(Gently)* Our Lord,

1,3: How majestic is your name in all the earth.

2,4,5: For with you is the fountain of life.

All: See! *(Pause)* The winter is past—

3: You have put gladness in my heart,

2: The rains are over and gone,

4: You have turned my mourning into dancing,

1: Flowers appear on the earth,

5: You have redeemed my life.

2: The season of

1,2: Singing has come!

3,4,5: Praise the Lord, oh my soul,

4: And all my inmost being,

1,2: Sing for joy,

3: To God our strength,

1: For he has loved us with an everlasting love.

All: Behold!

1: How great is the love the Father has lavished on us.

All: This is love:

5: Not that we loved God, but that he first loved us.

(Pause)

4: Therefore, in view of God's mercy, let love be your aim:

3: Be devoted to one another in love,

2: Preferring one another,

1: Following after love,

5: Encouraging one another daily,

4: While there is time—following after the things that make for peace.

1,3: And so may your love abound more and more in knowledge,

2,4: And in depth of wisdom.

5: By this shall all men know that you are my disciples—

1,3: My children,

2,4: My friends,

5: That you love one another.

All: Oh, Prince of Peace,

1,2: Surround us with songs of deliverance.

3: You are our hiding place,

4: Our shelter,

5: Our strength.

All: May your unfailing love rest upon us, oh Lord, even as we put our hope in you.

1,2: Hallelujah!

3: Christ is risen!

1,2: Hallelujah!

4: His Spirit remains!

1,2: Hallelujah!

5: The Lord God Almighty reigns!

All: Hallelujah!

1,2: Sing!

3,4,5: Sing!

All: Sing to the Lord! Amen.

15

Serve the Lord With Gladness

by
Deborah Gilmour Smyth

THEME: Serve the Lord with your whole heart and a willing mind

RUNNING TIME: Five minutes

CAST:

Reader 1 (man)
Reader 2 (woman)
Reader 3 (woman)
Reader 4 (man)

PRODUCTION SUGGESTIONS:

Props:
    Five uniform black notebooks

Costumes:
    Coordinated street clothes giving a clean, professional look

Serve the Lord With Gladness
THE SCRIPT

All: Shout joyfully to the Lord, all the earth!

Readers 1,4: Serve the Lord

All: With gladness.

Reader 2: Now, there was a man who had two sons. He went to the first and said,

Reader 4: *(Fatherly voice)* Son, go and work in the vineyard today.

Reader 2: But the son said,

Reader 3: No!

Reader 2: But later he changed his mind and went to work in the vineyard. Then the father went to the other son and said,

Reader 4: Son, go and work in the vineyard today.

Reader 2: And the son said,

Reader 1: Most certainly, dear father. I will go and work in the vineyard.

Readers 2,3,4: *(Looking at Reader 1)* But he didn't!

Reader 2: Now which of the two did what the father wanted?

Reader 3: Serve the Lord with gladness!

All: Extra! Extra!

1,4: Read all about it!

2,3: Exciting job opportunities!

All: Help Wanted!

1: Mechanics,

2,3: Students,

4: Loan officers,

3: Chemists,

1,2: Gardeners,

4: Philosophers,

1: Streetsweepers,

2: Poets,

4: Cooks,

2: Dressmakers,

3: Typists,

1,4: Fathers,

2,3: Mothers,

1,4: Sons,

2,3: And Daughters.

All: Countless career opportunities!

1,4: Serve the Lord with your whole heart,

2,3: And a willing mind,

1: For the Lord searches all hearts and understands every plan and thought.

2: Search me, oh God,

3: And know my heart.

2,3: Test me,

4: And see if there be any offensive way in me.

1: And lead me in the way everlasting.

All: *(Hushed)* Behold!

4: How great the love the Father has lavished on us.

All: This is love:

1: Not that we loved God, but that he first loved us.

2: Therefore, in view of God's mercy, let your love be sincere.

3: Be devoted to one another in brotherly love,

4: Preferring one another,

1: Following after love,

2: Encouraging one another daily.

3: Follow after things that make for peace:

4: Feeding,

1: Clothing,

2: Visiting,

3: Serving,

4: Caring.

1, 3: So that your love may abound

All: More and More in knowledge

1: And depth of wisdom.

2: By this shall all men know that you are my disciples—

2,4: My children,

2,3,4: My friends,

1: That you love one another.

All: Awaken in us new possibilities for service.

2,4: Kindle within us the fire of your compassion.

1,3: Let us be your Alleluia.

2,4: *(Softer echo)* Alleluia.

1: In this joyless, fragmented world,

All: Let us serve the Lord gladness!

1: Sing,

2: Sing,

3: Sing,

4: And be glad!

All: Sing!

2,3: And give him glory!

All: Serve the Lord—with gladness.